Dominican Moon

KEN NORRIS

Talonbooks
P.O. Box 2076, Vancouver, British Columbia, Canada V6B 3S3
www.talonbooks.com

Typeset in Garamond Book and printed and bound in Canada.

First Printing: 2005

 Canada Council Conseil des Arts
for the Arts du Canada · Canadä

The publisher gratefully acknowledges the financial support of the
Canada Council for the Arts; the Government of Canada through the
Book Publishing Industry Development Program; and the Province of
British Columbia through the British Columbia Arts Council for our
publishing activities.

LIBRARY AND ARCHIVES CANADA CATALOGUING IN PUBLICATION

Norris, Ken, 1951–
   Dominican moon / Ken Norris.

Poems.
ISBN 0-88922-526-5

   I. Title.

PS8577.O62D65 2005   C811'.54   C2005-902472-0

"Sinking only ends when you hit bottom, Arnold."
                    —Ms. Frizzle, *The Magic School Bus*

Praying for the heat and rain
To restore my soul again
                    —Eric Clapton, "My Father's Eyes"

I came back from those holiest waters new,
    remade, reborn, like a sun-wakened tree
    that spreads new foliage to the Spring dew

in sweetest freshness, healed of Winter's scars;
perfect, pure, and ready for the Stars.
                    —Dante Alighieri, *Purgatorio*

if you don't become the ocean
        you'll be seasick
            every day
                    —Leonard Cohen,
                    "Good Advice for Someone Like Me"

PROLOGUE

Discovery

I want to look at the world
from the angle of Columbus
discovering America,
and I don't really care
if Hispaniola isn't Cathay.

It seems to me
that what really matters
is making your way by the stars,
and having three ships.

KIRSI

(December 1996–January 1997)

SEEING THE STARS

Nighttime, ripped on rum,
knowing I'm in a garden again.
I can smell everything growing,
looking up I can see the stars.

Down at the beach
warm waves breaking,
no lights to interfere,
and the stars so bright, Orion
up so high, and one star, closer
to the horizon line, twinkling like mad.
That one, over there.

AFTER A RAIN

Warm drops have fallen
on the green fronds of the palms,
into the deep placid blue
of the hotel swimming pool.

The delicate flowers shimmer,
their red more red, purple more purple.
The cooled air breeds quiet,
and then the heat and noise
slowly rise up again.

CRICKETS

7:30 P.M. on New Year's Eve,
Bob Marley and the Wailers *Live!*
playing in the near distance,
the evening crickets
provide steady counterpoint.
I can't tie it to anything,
it is just phenomena,
and I just listen,
another fifteen minutes pass
before going out to dinner.

Feliz Año Nuevo

After a long Dominican New Year's Eve.
At twelve midnight
I kissed the beautiful girl of my dreams
square on the lips.

HAPPY NEW YEAR

When your new girlfriend's brother
is really drunk
and he is driving the motorconcho
the three of you are riding on
at four in the morning
on the newly christened New Year's Day
at top speed,
weaving in and out of
equally drunk traffic,
you may find yourself
inclined to become
suddenly romantic,
deeply religious
or highly philosophical.

KIRSI

A room in a foreign country.
Midnight. She moves me,
all the way to the other side
of that Muddy Waters song,
and far beyond.

*What is it about her
that moves you so deeply?*

Her beauty,
her dark beauty.

TRAVELLING

1.

A white table in a warm country.
Noon, and the palms trying to touch the sun.
The fire at its apex.

2.

She's in his head,
in his gut, the girl
from last night. She is
as placid as the sea
until aroused. Then
she rages and storms,
is the form of shipwreck
he desires.

3.

He swings in the hammock
of his dreams, sits
at the white table, drinking
agua minerale, intoxicated
with words, with life,
with the promise of a lover.

4.

The sky is talking to him
again, in blue, telling him
to live
before travelling out
into the endless universe.

A HOTEL ROOM IN SANTO DOMINGO

A hotel room at El Napolitano,
Kirsi passed out on the bed, kaput
from too much shopping. Out the window
the blue of the Caribbean Sea, green of cocopalms,
enough traffic on the Malecon to beat the band.
My mind's like the hotel swimming pool,
no one in it. Kirsi stirs. I wonder how long
it will take me to stop desiring her, how long
to cease to care.

        She touches me
in ways I've never been touched before.
Maybe it's her dark skin,
her braided hair. I don't know why
she moves me like the sky,
but she does, she does.

I can see the day but I don't know the day,
tied as I am to Kirsi's sleeping body.

Thinking of Stevens's palm
at the end of the mind, tropical philosophy.
It's too cold an intellect
that can't be melted down
by this tropic sun, and by a man's
unholy holy desires.

BETWEEN WORLDS

This first world poet
in the third world, ceiling fan
turning as the day heats up.

These pockets of strange life
are nowhere available
in the world he derives from,
and the third world offers him
anything he wants.

Anything
in the form of anything.

THE DECISION

Kirsi and I
are in bed.
I'm trying
to make myself
understood
in broken Spanish.
"Do you want to talk
or fuck?" she asks
in Spanish,
somewhat impatiently.
I choose
the latter.

LAST MORNING

"I want to be with you
for the rest of my life,"
she says to me in Spanish.
It's humbling, even
in a foreign language.

EIGHTEEN THINGS I LOVE ABOUT YOU

The way you move on the dance floor.
Your smile.
Your small breasts.
The scar on your left shoulder.
Your fondness for lambdi.
The way you hold a bottle of cerveza.
The way you pull my head down between your thighs.
How you walk.
Your lipstick smeared across my mouth.
Your taste in clothes (except for the red shoes).
How you feel in my arms asleep.
The intense welcome in your eyes.
The way you like being taken from behind.
The endless ropes of your hair.
Your handwriting.
The way you smoke cigarettes in bed.
How you hold my hand.
The way you say "Te amo."

QUESTIONNAIRE FOR DEPARTURE

Do you remember being breastfed?
What wild animal did you long to have for a pet?
Did you kill anything before the age of eight?
Did you ever smile at the moon?
How long did it take you to recover from your first broken heart?
Did you ever twinkle like a star?
Did you sleep with as many people as you could, as variously as you
    could?
Did you prefer alcohol, marijuana, kava, or betel nut?
Did red wine give you headaches?
Did you prefer clouds or horses?
How strongly did you like the taste of salt?
Did you ever get hopelessly lost in a foreign country?
Did you prefer pine trees or palm trees?
Did flowers make you feel amorous?
Did the ocean ever speak to you?
How many times did you feel like a hummingbird?
What did fear taste like?
What troubled you more: anxiety or boredom?
Were you ever fortunate enough to meet an alien?
Were you ever trifled with by earth spirits?
Given the opportunity, how would you have restructured time?
Did it seem to you that there was more life over the sea or under
    the sea?
Did you find the weather too hot or too cold?
Which of the four winds whispered too softly?
Did you like green tea or black tea?
What was more mysterious, rain or caves?
Given the contract, how would you have improved upon music?
Did the breaking dawn ever make you weep?
Were you more revulsed by snakes or centipedes?
Which seemed more terrible: a shark tank or a room full of clocks?
Did you have any sympathy for the rebel angels?
Which did you find more awful: unfulfilled desire or horseradish?
Did you ever curse the inventor of roller coasters?
Did you prefer ceiling fans or lobsters?

What was your favourite language to make love in?
What was the best thing about growing old?
Did you have a good time?

HAPPY HOUR

(March 1997)

Reflection

I like the high swaying palm trees at nighttime, and the stars.
I like the way the waves are breaking soundlessly
far out there on the reef. Now
just add a moon. We all go crazy here,
we all push the limits
of everything we've been. I'm maybe a little bit tired
of discovering all of these hungers
I didn't know I had.

The generator goes out
and the crickets emerge
with their fabricated song.
I'll go looking for romance
knowing romance is dead,
settle for some vestige of it.

There are worse fates
and worse codes of defeat.
After all this time
I've fallen hard
for the compensations.

THE SHOESHINE BOYS

I wave them off.
There must be
three hundred of them,
ages eight to fourteen,
all working the half-mile of tourist strip.
All putting their small fortunes together
five pesos at a time.

Lying Under the Fan

11:45 A.M., I am writing,
lying under the fan.
Stretched out across
a white-sheeted double bed.
Traffic rolls by, the day
heating up, the high palms
speaking to me of everything
the blue sky desires.
It desires so much.
I always thought it was placid
and calm, but it was always
like me, agitated
and full of longing. Longing
for the earth perhaps, longing
for the other. Where's Kirsi?
Not here yet. When will
the sky touch the earth?
Not now.

It is ever closer to noon,
and I am lying here,
lying across the clean white sheets
like a lonely word upon a page,
an autonomous word, a word
that has learned to feed itself
because it must, and yet
can still offer meaning.

What word it is
I cannot say,
but I am lying here
and the fan is turning.

SOURCE

Derived out of Mother Africa,
we were meant for warmer weather,
some, nevertheless, pushing north
to put on animal skins,
lose melanin, even inhabit
the frozen uninhabitable. Every time
I arrive in tropic islands
I know I'm returning to source.

BARCELÓ

I decide to get drunk
for a change. My agent
of change is
Barceló Añejo
Ron Superior, 34%
alcohol. Made locally.
And it goes down
like old-time firewater,
and I am twenty years
out of practice.

But after a while
I have a good buzz on,
a warm glow
in my esophagus, the dark essence
of the Dominican Republic
in my blood.

ART GALLERY BREAKFAST

Rainy Sunday morning.
This is what I do with my loneliness,
this is what I do with my love.
Last night I stumbled beneath the cocopalms
lost in a rum reverie, lost
in the dream of a love
that always fails to materialize.
She's somewhere in the distance.

I swat at the flies, watch the human traffic
go by, it is different,
it is the same, here in the green world.
We walk beneath the eternity of those stars
but once, longing for the bold transformations
of love with all our hearts.

EARLY MORNING

Early morning, a bird's striking song.
I remember the 7:00 A.M.s of Tahiti
when I was broken by a marriage
that totally fell in on me.
Now I am tired, hungover, and somewhat
disoriented by the return I've made.

Today I'll change hotels
and hope for a new room, a new outlook,
a significant change in my luck.
I'll even hope to see her face
though, right now, I have no idea
what to do with her.

KIRSI APPEARS

Kirsi appears.
Totally new hair.
I miss the old hair.
But still almost faint
watching her walk away.

OUT THERE

Out at the end of the pier,
closer to the waves,
totally surrounded by blue-green water.
I watch the banana boat
go by, a snorkeller
thrashing in the water.
The breeze never stops blowing,
clanking the riggings
of the moored sailboats,
and the sky and sea
never end.

THE BUSINESS OF SAND

The kids are playing down on la playa
with their buckets and pails,
completely caught up
in the business of sand.
Castles and strange constructions,
making something out of the randomness
the beach presents. Human enterprise.

And we all know
what happens
when the tide comes in.

Watching Kirsi Sleep

Kirsi
gives me
a Spanish lesson.
Then
we fuck.

Now she's totally wrapped up
in the top sheet, but before
half her naked body was covered
and half revealed, I sat on the floor
beside the bed and marvelled
at her contours, the way
nature perfected itself
in the sculpting of her body.
She added the nose ring,
the navel ring, the close-cropping
of her dark hair. I was glad
to be given that moment
in which to be the man
who looks at her
lying peacefully asleep in his bed, and knows
that he's been blessed.

GETTING MY PHOTO TAKEN WITH SEVERAL TORONTO BLUE JAYS PROSPECTS

It's a long walk out of Boca Chica
to the Blue Jays' baseball camp facility
far on the other side of the highway.
Along the way Peter and I talk
about our divorces, various girlfriends,
what it's like being here.
We pass houses, we pass
free-ranging goats and horses,
we cross railroad tracks,
walk long stretches of hot green nothingness,
two middle-aged men
with divorces behind them,
one a photographer, the other a poet,
walking in the hot sun
to a Dominican field of dreams.

When we arrive we find
two major-league-sized fields,
lush green and beautifully manicured.
Turns out it's a joint facility
for the Blue Jays and the Arizona Diamondbacks.
On one field
the prospects for the Diamondbacks
are going through fielding practice,
on the other
the Dominican prospects for the Blue Jays
are milling around.

Peter and I walk over to the Toronto field,
the players look at us,
and then six of them come walking over.
One of them speaks good English.
I tell him I'm from Toronto.
He says he could tell that I'm Canadian.
I ask him if any of them are currently playing
in the minor leagues, and he says that

every year four or five players from the camp go,
go to North America to play in the minor leagues,
and that they can come to the camp for three years,
and if they don't make it in that time, that's it.
Peter asks if he can take their picture, they say yes
and pose. One of the players waves me over.
I get my photograph taken
with six Toronto Blue Jays prospects.
After the photographs, I tell the guys
I'm looking forward to seeing them
play in Toronto in three years.
Then we all smile and say Adios.

La Criolla

Another morning sitting
at La Criolla, waiting
for breakfast to be served,
the Latin music
filling the air. For years
I hated this kind of music,
and now I have a strange affection for it.
Just as I now have a strange affection
for the Republica Dominicana,
and something of a desire to leave it.

Mar Caribe

Eight in the morning,
sitting in the sand, looking out
over the Caribbean Sea, full yellow sun
already burning low in the sky. Blue water,
waves breaking upon the reef. And I
am looking south to what? Venezuela?
This warm sea with its islas,
its vacationers, its distorted societies.
And what does the sea care? It has
its salt and its eternity, colourful fish
and unfathomable depths. We appear
and disappear like smoke, the taste
of salt and stars in our mouths.

LARRY AND ANDY

I don't know why
but Larry, the fifty-one-year-old excessively-friendly American,
keeps calling me Andy (I told him my name, several times).
I don't know why
but I no longer bother trying to correct him.
Everywhere we go he introduces me to everyone
as Andy, and I say hi.
So a lot of people here now know me as Andy.
All day long, whenever I see Larry
on the beach or by the hotel pool, it's
"How you doing, Andy?"
"What's happening, Andy?"
"Look at the tits on that one, Andy,"
and other terms of endearment.
For the guy I could be, but am not.
Still, I now answer to the name Andy,
and Andy agrees with Larry on just about everything.
Even if I personally disagree, Andy agrees.
"So what do you make, Andy? About fifty grand a year?"
"Yeah, Larry, about fifty grand."
"Look at the ass on her, Andy,
she could keep you going all night."
"Yeah, Larry, she really could."
Never have I been this agreeable.
Andy's an incredibly agreeable guy.
I don't know why
but I've finally met a fellow human being
I'm willing to tell
just exactly what he wants to hear.

TROPICAL RAIN

(June 1997)

DAYS

I know them again:
days with the length of days.
All of the minutes divided evenly,
symmetrical in the tropical breeze.

IL GABBIANO

I sit with the Italians
at Il Gabbiano, a seaside restaurant.
They smoke cigarettes
and talk a mile a minute
in a language I can't understand.
I write quickly in my notebook
about the blue of the sky, aquamarine water,
surrounding phenomena.
They are, perhaps, my people.

PARADISE

Yeah, it's a little vacant;
sometimes I'm a little vacant.
That's what the paradise experience
is all about. When you're not
being overwhelmed by the sublime
you're being exercised
in perfect emptiness.

In the Cool of the Evening

I sit an hour
in the cool of the evening,
swaying palms overhead,
looking for the first star.
There's the moon
in the darkening blue,
almost full. An hour ago
I wanted to say
the most outrageous things
to a girl I barely knew.
Barely know how
to be touched
by any of this.

WHO'S THAT GIRL?

Who's that girl
who walked through my evening,
fully present, dazzling,

holding everything back from me?
What's it matter?
She wants nothing
to do with me,

no matter what I say,
no matter who I leave,
no matter what I promise.

And I'll promise her anything.

And she won't give me anything.
I'd have to beg her for a smile.

Still,
she *did* tell me her name.
Stefani.

Which I'm clinging to
like an anchor.

POEM

Write the words
that say it all.

I'm lost
in the sky
and the blue
of the swimming pool.

Whoever I was
isn't coming back.

What can I distill
from this? The essence
of a red hibiscus flower.

TRUJILLO

Ray's grandfather
was one of the ones
who assassinated Trujillo.

Three years later
Ray's grandfather was killed.

Ray's mother
went into hiding
in the U.S.
for thirty-one years.

Now she's home,
cooking in the kitchen
of Ray's restaurant,
still looking worried.

Last evening she told me that,
after the assassination attempt,
when they rushed Trujillo
to the hospital, trying to save him,
the doctors couldn't find his head.

Then she shrugged her shoulders
and went back into the kitchen
to cook my dinner.

BROKEN MORNING

Another broken morning. I don't fuck
Kirsi in the mirror anymore, my secret life
is public news, the waters of the swimming pool
ever blue. And the sky. The sky
haunts me with its purity.
I want to be a red hibiscus flower
growing here in the sun.

SONG

Okay, poet, earn your keep.
Tell us why the sky isn't crying,
why the little fish
in the aquamarine waters
dart and swerve. The holiness
of worldly existence
has been crushed beneath the weight
of a material longing.
Ask your tired brain for visions,
ask your broken heart for a song.
Un cancion, por favor.
So that we can live forever
within the frame
of its pure delight.

POEM

How disappointing!
To have it all evaporate.
I wanted to write something
with the odd insubstantiality of clouds,
but all I managed to do
was to create smoke.

IN THE TROPICS

I am in the tropics again,
losing my religion,
losing my vision of the stars.
It's a John Donne bed,
the hot sun dragging itself
across the sky. Whenever
it speaks to me I look up
from my intense concentration
upon the body of this woman,
to catch a glimpse
of a transforming day
moving from morning
to afternoon to evening,
the intensity of the embrace
momentarily changing,
and the air heavy
with the weight of flowers.

IN THE END

In the end
we blew up
over a love we both claimed
but couldn't prove.

I was sad
to see her go, and relieved.

I reentered my own solitude,
closed my eyes and slept deeply,
her smile the sunrise
of my next and every morning.

JENNY

(August 1997)

PURPOSE

I could have made nobler choices,
could have decided to produce
something the world actually wants.
But this is what I wanted:
to be a keeper of the written record
of escaping time.

The sweet formality
of this enterprise.
The deep familiarity.

The distances we cover
in order to arrive.

LANDSCAPE

There used to be more trees
in my poems, more cocopalms,
more aquamarine seas. Correlatives,
objective or otherwise. Then
tiredness got to me, and I tried
to stop painting the world.
The world doesn't need my praise.
What does? The faint glimmer
of hope still visible on the horizon.

The Mornings

The mornings are nice
before the heat is turned on
and the air becomes heavy
with the smell of burnt suns.

For now the breeze is cool
and I inhabit a benign green world
based entirely upon sleeplessness
and fluttering yellow butterflies.

For three mornings
I've sat on this park bench
waiting for Maria.

And now
I understand Beckett
just a little more.

JENNY

How could I resist her?
She looks so beautiful in certain lights.
And what I see in her eyes
I've never seen before.

The glue of my life
evaporates. I fall apart
like a man who has gone past
his tequila limit.

WATCHING JENNY SLEEP

Sometimes I'm overwhelmed.
Now I'm just watching Jenny sleep.
I don't know who she is
or why she has this power to move me.
Last night she had me so aroused
I started laughing out loud,
it was all so fabulous and ridiculous.
It must have something to do
with those long legs of hers,
and her eyes that are so dark
I can't find a colour for them.

FALLING

In bed
I pour myself into her,
put everything I have
into every nuance, every caress.

Out of bed
I try talking sweetly to her,
walking my tightrope
of broken Spanish.

IN LOVE AGAIN

She's asleep in my bed again,
dreaming her wandering dreams.
How long I dreamed of her,
and then one day she simply
washed up on the shoreline
of my senses. Oh my,
it's love again, and who am I
to argue?

HAPPY IDIOT

Weeks go by
and I don't pick up a pen.

Don't need to.
Why bother.

I'm falling
deeper and deeper
into realms of happiness,
days of calm.

I'm no longer a poet.
Just Jenny's lover.

FOR JENNY

Everything touches me:
your aspirin, your cigarettes.
My eyes are filled with regret
and wonder, abject wonder
that you could love me.

THE LIGHTENING SKY

Morning, and I am
headed home. Heat
of the airport, and
the lightening sky.
All of last night's
boundless passion
dead on arrival.

To Jenny

The otherness of you.
Your depths of Spanish, your modelo height.
The intoxicating darkness of your eyes.
The way your smile breaks into light
like a sunrise. The patience
of Indian peoples that your whole being
wears. The gifted access you give me
to the feminine world.
The shadows that criss-cross your heart
as you speak of loss.
The strength of your weathered hands.
Your surrender. The way
you ride me through the dark.
One lost earring that is falta.
The other earring you gave to me
in remembrance of what we found
among the kisses and the ravaged flowers.
No mas lagrimas, y la última noche.

SPANISH HEADACHE

(October–November 1997)

FOR JENNY

I see you again
and love evaporates.

We make non-stop love
for three hours
and love evaporates.

You keep talking to me
in patient Spanish
and love evaporates.

I send you home
in the morning light
and love evaporates.

You come back
in the afternoon,
talk to me
in passionate Spanish
for three hours,
loving me with your eyes.

We take off our clothes,
our histories,
our preconceptions,
and make love.

And love is affirmed.

Every Time

Every time we make love
I lose myself a little more.

Every time we make love
I desire you a little more.

One day you'll mean
everything to me,
and there will be nothing
left of me.

Return

I returned to you on a gambler's whim,
knowing the chances weren't good.
I fell asleep in your arms anyway,
no longer angry. I gave myself
a Spanish headache endlessly talking to you.

These are the things that matter
and don't matter, these are the years
of tearing it all down
to figure out how it works.

Spanish Is the Loving Tongue

You say the most outrageous things
when we're making love,
and half of them I don't even understand.

Still, I wouldn't miss this
for half the profits
of the English-speaking world.

GONE TO SANTIAGO

Jenny's gone to Santiago.
To visit her family.
While she's away
she wants me to think about
marrying her.
What's to think about?
I've only been divorced a year.
And I've only known her for two months.
What's the rush?

Still, I can see
where this one's heading.
If you don't want to marry me
you don't really love me.
If you don't really love me
you're just playing around with me.
If you're just playing around with me
you're breaking my heart
and wasting my time.

How do I hold all of that off
and still keep her close to me?
With a woman this passionate,
tall, and beautiful,
a man needs a quick reaction time
and absolute answers.

THE PARK

Saturday morning, back in my park
with the green trees and red hibiscus.
Too little sleep, and now the heat of the day
seems almost friendly as it notches up
a degree every ten minutes.
I've come here to mourn
the death of the beautiful past,
and the green gripping present
is all around me, graced by a breeze.

THE POET, GOING DEEPER INTO HIS RESOURCES

It's no lie
that I live to write.
Believing in the alchemy of words,
exposure to this much
sand and sea and sky
has a tendency to erode language away,
or else reduce the poet
to an excessive use of descriptive superlatives.
The days are beautiful and hot
and dragging, I've chained myself to a model
of last year's man, and words
can't release me. They never could.

A New Way

Sleepy in the middle of the day,
and a dulled focus. This morning
I said goodbye to Lew and Stan, and then
this afternoon I said goodbye to Bill and Bill.
Now I'm here on my own, sitting
on a barstool, my playhouse
torn down, trying to imagine
a new way of being here.

DOING MY PAGES

I attempt to do my pages,
the air-conditioning blasting,
the poet in the mirror.
Outside, the heat surrounds.
It's one-thirty in the afternoon
and one could die of thirst.
All morning I've been imagining
a broken-hearted god.

The sweltering beach
folds everyone under, a sandcrab
scuttles for a place to hide,
and the day is divided
into equal portions.

MISSING JENNY

I miss her sleeping beside me,
miss her putting up
with my miserable Spanish.

She's gone away,
and here I am,
doing penance
for what sins?

NORTH, SOUTH, EAST, NO WEST

In Republica Dominicana
there is a north,
there is a south,
there is an east,
but there is no west (that's Haiti).

PANTHEON OF DOMINICAN BALLPLAYERS

Raul Mondesi wants the L.A. Dodgers
to pay him forty-five million dollars
for a five-year contract.
In Dominican pesos, that's 547.2 million pesos.
In a poor country like this
major league ballplayers live like gods.

JENNY RETURNS

Jenny finally comes down from Santiago.
Our kisses are sweet,
our lovemaking sweeter.
Only in the morning
does she start
to slowly apply pressure.

THE POET'S ALIBI

Sunday morning, Jenny's watching
pointless Dominican television,
the volume turned all the way up,
the air-conditioning blasting.
It's a loud life
whenever I'm with her.

I lie across the bed
exercising the poet's alibi.
For a while I don't have to feel
anything I don't want to,
don't have to confront
the present situation.
I can exist in a world
of my own creation,
and only in the background
is there the persistent sound
of her Dominican music.

I SAY

I say, no,
I can't marry you now.

I say, let's talk about this
in six months' time,
in a year's time.

I say, let's just see
what happens.

I say, I love you
but I need to be sure.

I say, can we stop
talking about this for a while.

I say, you have the most
beautiful eyes.

She says, *ciao, baby*.

She says, *adios*.

SURELY

Surely
she's coming back to me.

Surely
she's coming back to me
and will say, mi amor,
te amo,
I understand.

WINTER BASEBALL

I'm watching Dominican baseball on TV.
The Leones and the Aguilas are tied 4-4
after seven innings. I can't follow
what the commentators are saying at all.
But it is very fine baseball.

THE SITUATION

A year in and out of the Dominican Republic,
and the whole thing maybe winding down.
Tomorrow I fly back into the arms of America.
How I wish I could love it.

STARS OVER SANTIAGO

(January 1998)

BLESS YOU

Bless you, little rooster,
crowing my morning
into riot.

I have too many feelings
and a tired mind.
The Sunday poet
trying to come to terms
with Saturday night.

I'll work it out in poems:
my tiredness, my disappointment,
my loneliness.

I'll arise
out of these ashes too.

The ashes of Jenny,
what we shared.

MATERIAL

The landscape, the eyes,
the trees twisting into light.
Tourists passing by, and the people
living in the line of lights of the night game
in San Pedro. Blue park benches and naranjas,
car accidents and wandering black goats
that wind up as roadkill, the sweetness of water,
bitterness of estrangement, the green,
green, and green, and the last cup
of what I thought I wanted:
it is all material.

As a Young Man

As a young man
my mistake was in thinking
all of those writers were heroes.
They weren't. They were just
a bunch of lonely guys
who managed to take good notes.

Avenida Independencia

Santo Domingo. Avenida Independencia.
How I love this street
with its trees and shade,
its shade and trees,
the way the light falls,
the way the light has always fallen
here on the island of Hispaniola,
first outpost of a grand new world.

SANTIAGO

Jenny's city.
The place where she grew up
and grew into her life.
It is beautiful and lyrical
and has totally informed her.
A city of hills
and surrounding mountains,
poverty and refinement,
a city that's been transported out of time.
I love the elegance and roll of it.
Though she's gone
her city will stay and stay.

I'm holding on
to a warm breeze. It whispers
your name. When the rain
begins falling
the sky is crying
about the end of our love.

As the World Falls Away

Sitting in the sun
as the world falls away.
All those late nights,
and the world falling away.
The flowers still tempt me,
but the world goes on falling away.

SOSUA

There go those tropical crickets again,
counterpoint to the overhead ceiling fan.
Night comes down, and the coolness invades,
the trees in the garden almost stately.
I'll haul my bruised heart out into the evening,
determined to get over it.

She made love to me so sweetly,
and now I'm some asshole
wishing sex weren't quite so sweet,
wishing she were here
to get down on the floor again,
or to do it against the wall,
or straddling me in a rickety chair
before the knowing mirror.
She made a bed seem antiquated.

STANDING ROOM ONLY

It's standing room only
as the Aguilas play Escogido.
The stadium is packed
with rabid fanáticos
from both sides.
Arriving late, buying a ticket
from a scalper, I stand
through the last six innings
and it is wonderful, baseball
just the way I've imagined it could be:
passionate and joyful
underneath the lights,
underneath a warm half-moon.

LUNCH POEM

I can understand
the need for security
in banks, casinos,
and other places
where the big money is.
But why is there
a security guard
with a shotgun
monitoring the door here
at Burger King?

TO JENNY

I looked for your eyes in Santiago.
I tried to find a duplicate of you
walking in the streets of your city.
The women were beautiful
but they were not you.
And the eyes that looked back at me:
they failed to speak
in that dark passionate language of yours.

DOMINICAN MOON

You touch me when I'm warm,
my armour peeled away,
my heart open to your light.

You tug at me, tug at the water
lapping at my feet, kiss the sand
with lunacy and dog's breath.

The woman I am looking for,
the woman I can never find,
she is your avatar, she wears
the moon crown and the insubstantial veils
of your petalled light.

STEFANI

(March 1998)

You Could Look It Up

I just missed
by one day
a total eclipse of the moon.

Kismet

The last time I was here
I looked for Kirsi
for three days
with no luck.

This time
I bump into her
on the street
in five minutes.

WIPED OUT SECOND DAY

Jet-lagged and tired and hot
and totally disoriented, if the truth
be known. Quick sex with Kirsi
this morning hitting me like an errant oug-oug.
I'll spend twelve hours in bed
and get no sleep, just drift
to the sound of the generator,
lose myself in the turning blades
of the overhead ceiling fan.
She was here, and now she's gone,
and all tomorrow's promises
don't mean much.

The palm trees are everywhere
but I can't find them.
The green sea is walking in
to meet the shore,
but I can't reach it.
There's a blue sky overhead
but I don't see it.
I'm lost and lost
in tiredness, and in
the whole internal drama.

REVISION

Every day I revise my life.
The morning dawns, and possibility
spills out. The world is green
and wide and compellingly beautiful.
Things need to be re-envisioned
in the light of
this.

POEM

I am the quiet poet
raising a little Cain.

I am the night sky
smiling with its crescent moon.

I am the green waves
breaking and breaking.

My Secret Life

In the quiet of the morning
I organize my secret life.
There aren't many palm trees
in these poems, no palm
at the end of the mind.
No monkey and coconuts either.

Reading Wallace Stevens
at seventeen
set me on this path, this poet
in the tropics borne out of
my vision of that swaying palm tree.
I could see it in all of its abstraction,
and it became a woman as I approached it.

LAS TERRENAS

Countless cocopalms. Blue waves
coming in to kiss the tan sand.
In the night, under stars,
I stagger past a raging bonfire
on the beach, wanting to put my longing
to rest. Walking there, I remember
the young poet who headed for the South Seas
in search of the ineffable,
and kept calling it love. Eventually
love arrived, and still what he was searching for
eluded him, until he became me.

I remember all the South Seas days here,
how I wandered lonely as a cloud
looking for the island of my dreams.
I moved beneath the cocopalms in a trance,
climbed the green hills up into perfection.
Diamond Head, Upolu, Bora Bora—
they entered my heart
and now come back to me—here
in this green green place beside the sea.

THE WIND

The wind blowing in off the ocean,
the drift of clouds above the horizon line.

Sometimes I feel too much
in a place like this.

Driving out of Las Terrenas

Hard to believe all this rugged greenness
is real and in place, that it isn't being created
right now, mile upon mile, just to impress us.
The long road winds all the way down
to Sanchez, and I say a prayer
to the Dominican brake gods.

PARTY

The dancing goes on and on, and for once
I don't get a headache. It's four
in the morning and I am under the stars of Sosua,
on the back of a motorbike,
drunk on Anna, all six feet of her.
If I didn't take it so seriously
I'd laugh out loud, at the absurdities
of human desire, and how we fall into beds
so achingly and open. Who cares
that the motorconcho guy is gay,
and keeps grabbing my leg, wanting me
to fuck him? We all have desires,
and they all seem sane to us.
Or insane, the moment in the party
when you give yourself over to it,
and allow yourself to be thrown just about anywhere.

FINITO

The 5:00 A.M. crickets tell me
Jenny's never coming back my way.
That rooster crowing is trying to tell me
everything is finished.
I've been giving her up, I've been
hoping against hope, I've been bargaining
with the universe for just a few more hours
of gratified desire. Sometimes
it's good to admit your defeat,
and I'll admit it now, here,
in this hotel room in Sosua, in the early morning
with the ceiling fan turning overhead.
I'll never touch her again,
never again be rocked by her
like the sweet ocean.
It's finished, I'm empty,
I'll be needing a new horizon.

DOMINICAN MOON

How many times will I walk this winding road
wondering where it all went wrong?
The trees twist up into the night,
and there is a light wind blowing.
The motorconchos come and go, their small engines
whispering of illicit pleasures.
Love is lost, or sex is found
and then lost again, everything
sliding with the soul into a limbo-like
kind of oblivion. I am a man
walking nowhere, walking home, back to his hotel,
and it is late, late, three or four
in the morning, the music in my head
winding down, the sweet vacancy of morning
a couple of hours away. I don't own
any of it, not one speck of the universe,
am just a traveller, passing through.
And all this walking, misery, lostness, despair,
all of it is taking place
under a late night full Dominican Moon.

INCIDENT

I was there that morning
when the five Dominican guys
pushed the red car
that had gotten stuck in the sand
out of the ocean.

STEFANI

Remember her reticence?
She stood there
in the warm shadows of evening
telling you why
it was never going to happen.

She had a good long list
of your faults
and your indiscretions,
was totally convinced
you were wholly insincere.

That was a year ago.
And now she's lying
in your bed asleep,
and what has changed
besides yourself?

THE SEVENTH FLOOR OF THIS HOTEL

Will we ever be getting out of bed?
Believe me, I'm far from complaining.
The days start late,
and turn into night soon enough,
and we hot-wire the diurnal,
turn it all into passionate night anyway,
even when the sun is banging at the window,
even when the maid service
is knocking at the door.
I think we slipped out for a cappuccino once
so they could change the sheets.
Then we soon came back
to our amorous work.

I know I'm leaving one morning,
and that morning is coming soon enough.
I'm trying hard not to see it
out of the corner of my eye.
I'm just trying to stay stuck and focused here
on the seventh floor of this hotel.

BÉISBOL ROMÁNTICO

(April–June 1998)

SPRING

for Stefani

It's Spring in the terrestrial world
and I have this photograph of you.

Memories, too,
fine memories.

But only a single photograph.
How much can I find there?
I won't look into your alive eyes
for months yet.

You on your island
and me on mine,
surrounded by all these alligators
one finds in a wilderness suburbia.

All the losses
of all the failed existences.

Call the number I gave you.
Let me hear your voice again.

Or tell your photograph
to come to life
and hold me close.

THE LONG HAUL

The long haul
to the island paradise
that isn't paradise
but, in a pinch,
will have to do.

On the beach
I'll remember eternity
as the waves crest and break.

Too often
what we're thinking about
is time, time, time,

when it's in eternity
we'll be spending
almost all our time.

ANOTHER MORNING IN THE WORLD

I'll go for a walk along the beach
before the day heats up, maybe even
go for a swim, lie there a while
as the sun climbs up
to the twelfth meridian.
Don't get me wrong, I'm grateful
for my life, even if, at times,
I do despair. But I
have never asked for a refund,
and I'm certainly not
asking for one now.

COURTSHIP

I haven't seen Stefani.
No one's seen Stefani.
I know she's somewhere
on this island.

How does anyone manage
to do courtship successfully
in a country without telephones?

WHILE I'M HAVING BREAKFAST

She empties
the blue plastic pail
full of water,
fills it up again
from the tap
beside the Pepsi sign,
carries it back to the shop.

Darling,
your everyday life
is my exotica.

NEWS OF JENNY

In La Criolla last night
Matilde told me
that Jenny married
a tall German fellow
a month ago,
and is now living in Germany.

I believe it.
She was stunning.
Someone was bound to marry her,
and soon.

BÉISBOL ROMÁNTICO

The early professional days,
the early fifties,
before alliances were forged
with American teams.

It was when
Dominicans owned
their own sport
and played for pride alone.

BASEBALL

Despite all the winding turns
of innings, and
various strategies,
there's an innate simplicity
at the heart of the game.

A simplicity that I admire.

You're up
and the pitcher pitches the ball.
Four balls, you walk.
Three strikes, you're out.

ODE TO SLEEP

Oh Sleep,
how you elude me sometimes,
leaving me nothing
but the broken night,
the broken morning.
No rest. No dreams.
And I pay for my excesses
in tiredness,
moving out to the perimeter
of hallucination, and I drag
my sorry self
through hours I have no hope
of ever making mine.

Other times you are sweetness itself,
and I enter you deeply,
dream, and awaken refreshed.
All night my head
is filled with running horses,
easy breezes, everything
colliding
in an atmosphere
of unpredictable coincidence.

With you, Sleep,
it is really
all or nothing.

ROULETTE

I hang around in the casino
playing roulette. Everyone
is more wasted than I am.
I observe once again
that there are never any clocks in casinos.
They want you to believe
that, by winning, you can stop time.

SPEAKING SPANISH

I've led this whole other life
that's taken place in Spanish.

When I was with Jenny
I made the greatest love declarations.

I used words
like corazon and alma,
amor and siempre,
without any embarrassment at all.

Message

Your great poems
are waiting for you
in a suitcase
marked "Asia."

A Lesson in Cultural Relativism

Last night tall Matilde
stopped me on the street
and started berating me
for my worn jeans.

When you're poor
you do your best
to look presentable.

Only in the first world
do we consciously
dress like bums.

CUTTING CANE

In the early 1980s
the Dominican Republic
closed its border with Haiti
yet once again.
This meant there were no Haitians
to harvest the sugar cane.

Some ballplayers tried to mobilize
the Dominicans
by declaring "The People's Cane Harvest."
With the press covering their actions,
the ballplayers went out into the fields,
rolled up their sleeves and, with machetes,
started hacking away at the cane.
Thousands of Dominicans had gathered
to watch, but not one of them
lifted a hand to help.
They just laughed with dumbstruck awe.
Never before had they seen rich Dominicans
do such a ridiculous thing.

Nueva York

Everyone here believes I live in Nueva York.
I tell them Maine, but they figure Maine
is just a part of Nueva York.
They all dream of going to Nueva York.
Some have relatives there.
A few used to live there
before they got deported for selling drugs.
Most seem to think that Nueva York
is three times the size of Texas,
and is something of a Latin paradise.
I guess it is.
When they speak to me of Nueva York
I listen intently.
The way they describe it,
it sounds so interesting.
I'd really like to go there sometime.

ODE TO THE CARIBBEAN SEA

I've watched the moonlight
dance over your dark surface,
the warm full moon
disperse upon your waters.
And always the inclining cocopalms
were hovering above. I've kissed lovers
on your sandy shoreline, walked hand-in-hand
with exciting newly-met strangers
along your periphery. You are
the nighttime sea, the sexual sea,
the ganga sea, the sea I have sailed
my heart upon.

POEM

Where's Kirsi,
where's Jenny,
where's Stefani?

Somehow
I wind up
in the arms of Matilde,
wanting to forget.

CULTURAL EXCHANGE

Luis asks me if I like the Dominican Republic.
Oh yes, I say. I like Dominican baseball,
I like Dominican music, I like Dominican food,
I like Dominican culture.
That's funny, Luis says, because I like
American culture and American music.
But I don't like American food.
Why not? I ask.
It's too unnatural, artificial.
I like Italian food, Luis declares.

To Jenny, in Germany

I think of you, often.
I think of you with tenderness
and affection, ardour and candour.
Don't think I didn't care,
or didn't care enough.
Te amo mucho, and
I remember everything.

VIDA ALTA

(November–December 1998)

ARRIVAL

With fanfare,
with one hundred angels dancing
to a throbbing disco beat,
with lights swirling,
with a sky of stars
and a rumour of rainbows,
with all the books of love
jubilantly conversing,
with the night pulsing like oysters
and Cuba Libres going to one's head,
with shadows peeled back by a shattering light,
Stefani arrives.

REPRIMAND

When she's in my arms
she asks,
"Why didn't you come
looking for me?"

"I was looking for you,"
I say, "I looked
everywhere for you."

"Then why didn't
you find me?"

In Your Eyes

I love looking into your eyes.
I love the crazy kind
of light I find there.
And everything that's reflected.

What's reflected?
The ceiling, the sky,
the room, the stars,
the light burning beside the bed.
In your eyes
the only thing I never see
is myself.

BALCONY SCENE

I'm endlessly
falling into you.

Your dark eyes,
your boundless brown curls.

The sky's
losing its light,

the tree leaves
becoming endarkened shadows.

You're standing out
on the balcony,

for a change
wearing clothes.

Blue blouse,
red pants.

A warm evening breeze
kissing us.

I'm standing
five feet away from you.

Too far.

THE CALM AFTER

Evening falling again.
The air warm and scented with flowers.
We're out on the balcony,
you're wrapped in a towel,
smoking a joint, laughing lightly.

I like watching the smoke
coil and drift
off into the upper evening air,
like the whiff I get of it,
sitting here beside you.

The quiet idyllic life,
the calm after
the latest sexual storm,
in this hour
before the evening meal.

In ten minutes
you'll get up
and start to go about
picking clothes, doing make-up,
time in the mirror,
getting ready for the world.

I like this moment
more than anything,
the smoke drifting,
the conversation not going
anywhere in particular,
light smoking, light talking,
the relative absence
of clothes, the occasional
"mi amor" and kiss,
as the earth transitions
into warm darkness.

GARDEN OF LOVE

It's only the two of us
in this world we're discovering,
world we're making,
garden of love we find ourselves in.

This room becomes a world,
and no one else exists.
I'm alone with you for hours,
following where you lead me:
into moments of delight,
moments of laughter,
of deep Hispanic passion,
deeper pleasures.

What was I doing
before you came into existence?
Nothing much.
Naming animals,
walking around.

FALLING

So I tumble
into the old nets,
my senses closed
to everything that is not you.

To everything that does not involve you.
Whatever that might be.

ODD NIGHT

And then you say to me,
"Let's get high tonight.
Let's get really high."

I thought we already were.
On love and desire.
On one another.

"Just a little coca.
It'll feel really good."

I'm already feeling really good.
In the pocket. Relaxed.

I don't want coke.
You want coke?
Fine.

Not fine.
Not really.

And when you've performed
your ceremony,
arranged lines on the glass tabletop,
offered me lines, snorted lines
using a twenty-peso note,

when you're really high,
lying on the bed, laughing,
talking rapid-fire Spanish
I'm having a hard time following,

it's become an odd night,
and I get restless, tired, bored.
As you go on talking and talking,
I fall asleep
without making love to you.

STEPPING OUT

I step out
into the afternoon
while you sleep,
visit the green world.

It's all going along
very well without us.

THE SADNESS OF YOUR SMILE

I never noticed
the sadness of your smile before.
With all the passion
and the mayhem, with all the joy
of you returning to my arms,
I never noticed the formality
that underlies your smiling.
As if you don't really believe in it.

Oh, when you're loud and rolling,
dragging me here, throwing me there,
pulling me down on the bed after you,
there's that moment
of having me
right where you want me,
off-balance and hungry,
enthralled and engaged.
And then you're happy,
and then your proud smile breaks free.

But this morning
when everything was quiet,
you caught me
looking at you
while you were looking at yourself in the mirror,
and I watched the curtain come up
on your surprised smile,
the smile you needed to put on.
And it was off-balance and sad,
as if you had to compensate for
secrets you could never tell,
as if you knew something
infinitely sorrowful about life,
as if you knew the world
in ways the world should never be known.

PAST AND PRESENT

She's intimated
a former rock star boyfriend
introduced her
to the fast high life.

She sure does know
how to order up room service,
and where to send out
for the full range of drugs.

River

She seems to be having fun
mixing cocaine with a little speed.

Already the marijuana smoke
hanging in the air
is taking me back twenty years,

and it's nice to have
a buzz on
when we make love.

And she's generous
with her drugs and affection,
keeps offering me
smooth lines of anything I want.

And I feel like jumping in.
I'm getting tired of standing
on this side of the river.

TEMPTED

It's always a minute
from a taste
to a more abundant meal.

Pretty soon
you're chowing down
on ecstasy,

happy to be losing yourself
in her arms,
in the wallpaper,

high on
whatever it is,
and desire.

Lost in the old
tried and true
formulation.

The same old tree,
the same apple,
the same temptation.

GOING

I thought we were here
trying to build
something to remember.

But it's very clear
there's something or someone
she's trying to forget.

And wherever it is
she's going in the fallen world,
she wants company.

SLIDE

The way things
keep getting wound up,
it's getting harder and harder.

I wanted to be in love,
not doing time
trying to unload
the various addictions,
the seven deadly sins.

I'm losing space,
in danger
of losing perspective,
sliding right back into
a very old familiar way of life.

I need Stefani
to come back into her senses,
to scuttle the crazed mission,
to get straight for one day
and hold me in her arms.

THE SWIMMER'S MOMENT

I'm not the strongest of swimmers.
And the water around here
is getting deeper and deeper.

How I'd like to rescue her,
and be her hero. But it's getting
to the point where,
if I swim out to her,
she's going to panic,
and we're both
going to wind up drowned.

What's Interesting

What's interesting to me
is you.

Not coca,
not la vida alta.

Not speeding through the night
forgetting to make love.

I didn't really enjoy
these kinds of conversations
in English,
never mind in Spanish.

Though my language skills
are improving.

But love is dying
everywhere around us,

and I didn't come all this way
just to lose you like this.

STEFANI,

Don't leave me
standing here,
wishing it were otherwise.

I need you
to be present, not absent,
need you to be here
in mind and feeling
as well as in body.

I don't need you
to be calling me
toward the rocks.

You're tearing this love apart,
tearing me apart,
and I don't have the fortitude
to marry you
and see you through rehab.

And what other chance do we have?

For Christ's sake,
stop being in love
with oblivion,
and wake up
to the man beside you.

LAST MORNING

On the slimmest of pretexts,
I grease the skids under her
and slide her out the door.

I'll be missing her
for as long as I miss her,
but I can't live like this anymore.

AFTERMATH

(January–June 1999)

DOMINICAN LITANY

I was your shoeshine boy
Give me twenty pesos
I need to take a motorconcho
Give me twenty pesos
I'm hungry for a hamburger
Give me twenty pesos
I want a cerveza
Give me twenty pesos
The hurricane destroyed my house
Give me twenty pesos
I am, as you know, your first girlfriend's sister
Give me twenty pesos
Today is my birthday
Give me twenty pesos
My grandmother needs a hysterectomy
Give me twenty pesos
I am fat and menacing
Give me twenty pesos
My uncle caught a walleyed fish
Give me twenty pesos
I lost my coca in the sand
Give me twenty pesos
I was a shark in a previous lifetime
Give me twenty pesos
My heart is in the compraventa
Give me twenty pesos
I am the avatar of divine love
Give me twenty pesos

THE PURSUIT OF HAPPINESS

The pursuit of happiness
is making me blue.
How about you?
Maybe we should be chasing
something else.

MORNING IN THE TROPICS

That rooster's been crowing
for a thousand years.
And now the cool of the morning
surrounds him. The birds
start to sing. It's green
and green and green
out there in the world,
and the blue sky
doesn't want to ally itself
with anything.

NEXT DOOR

When Stefani
went supernova
it broke my heart.

Proving
I still have one.

I live next door now to my old life.

When I lived next door
she was out on my balcony
and in my bed.
She was calling and calling my name.

Now I don't have a balcony,
and I sleep alone.

MY NEW LIFE

I hang around in casinos
and play roulette.
I speak Spanish.
I collect women.
In love and gambling
I know when to quit.

LOVE SONG

I am working my way down
to my Hispanic roots,
and when I say "I"
I mean all of this.
From the frozen wastelands of Baffin Island
to the difficult beauty of Patagonia,
I have a Spanish soul.
You can proclaim that it's all America,
but I think it would be better
if you called me Alma.
And when you call,
call tenderly, and with love.

SENTIMIENTOS

for Stefani

You've pitched a tent in the middle of my affections
and I couldn't get you out with dynamite.
Nor with any other ploy. I've tried
jamming my own radar, and still it's darkly fixated
upon you. Weeks go by, even months,
and still the queen of hearts keeps coming up you.
Your wild mane of hair, your hyper-accelerated oral technique—
they're enshrined in my own personal sexual hall of fame.
To say nothing of your eyes. A twelve-minute song
couldn't begin to invoke them, or speak to their giddy sadness.
My love, you *are* my love,
for I guess I am eternally stuck on you.
Blow me a kiss from the top of Cocaine Mountain
and I'll try to square your accounts with the dealers.

FOLD

Another tropical morning that almost fails to reach me,
but those birds are persistent, and so is the sun,
so now I am grateful, and still a little sad.
This hotel is haunted by the ghost of a great love.
I don't doubt that I still dream of her, all night long
go reaching for another lonely chance.
It's her absence that keeps insistently
calling to me. And might I add
that I threw her out one morning,
and the look on her face was the embodiment of startled.
She thought she had my full attention,
and she did, but the pain I was in
wouldn't let me go another hour with her, another mile.
It was a desperate high-stakes game I was playing,
and all I could do at that moment was fold.

VISUAL RECORD

It's one of those days when the sky never clears.
And every hour or two: rain.
Right now the brightly-coloured umbrellas are out,
and the black and white couples move along the humid street
wondering what to do next. I should
have had my photograph taken more often.
There is almost no visual record
of my ever having been here.

DIGAME

The sun's setting
on the century,
on these times, it's all
in the public domain now.
We lose ourselves in Latin rhythms.

My luck has changed.
I keep losing at the Big Casino.

Digame, speak to me,
beneath the evening's
swaying palm trees.

Tell me which way
to go now.

DOMINICAN MOON

Composed like a dark novel-in-verse, *Dominican Moon* is the second book in Ken Norris's poetic travel trilogy. With Dante as his guide, he leaves behind the predominantly European terrain of the first book in this series, *Limbo Road*, and finds himself in the "terra incognita" of the Caribbean Sea.

On his own contemporary voyage of discovery of the island of Hispaniola, the "new world" Columbus discovered in 1492, Norris encounters seductive lovers and moon-haunted tropical nights, dark Dominican rum and winter baseball, sugar cane fields and "the city of shortstops."

At the heart of the book is an unsettling story of the deficiencies of love—of a perhaps not so divine comedy of those who didn't love enough—steeped in a clash of cultures wherein the third world willingly, even perversely, offers itself up as a farm-team for the first, fueled by the cataclysm of that other third world export, cocaine.

"From all [of Ken Norris's] books taken together I get a better sense, a tragic and painful sense, of the age we are living in than I do from the daily and nightly broadcasts of world news ... And in all this he is profoundly original, open and vulnerable, with a unique personal note that speaks to the heart of the reader."
—Louis Dudek, *Poetry Canada*

$17.95 Canada / $15.95 USA
ISBN 0-88922-526-5

51595

9 780889 225268

Cover design by Adam Swica